Body Talk

CW00859150

Body Talk

Charley Barnes

Picaroon Poetry
Sheffield, UK

Picaroon Poetry
Sheffield, United Kingdom

ISBN 978-0-244-21546-0

Cover image is by Jack Antal via Unsplash, and used under the CC0 Public Domain License.

Book and cover designed by Kate Garrett/Picaroon Poetry.

To Harriet,
thank you for telling me to write about it

Self-portrait of the writer

Naked, I stand in front of my floor-to-ceiling mirror. There is a chair wedged beneath the handle of my bedroom door, so I know that we won't be disturbed.

In red lipstick, I write 'Bingo wing' along the inside of my outstretched arm's reflection. I follow the line of too-obvious veins across my chest, up to my clavicles, and I use this as a guide to write 'Not obvious enough' along both collar bones. Around each breast I draw a bright red circle and sketch 'Too saggy now' beneath them, along my sternum; I've heard that this is where all the girls are getting their tattoos.

Edging closer to my stomach – smaller than it was but strained beyond repair – with my lipstick I outline old stretchmarks until lines dance across my belly, as though my skin has been licked by thin flames. In a smaller font I add a collage of insults – 'fat', 'chubby', 'squishy' – until my abdomen is a mass of words. I move down to my legs...

When the work is finished I put my clothes back on, turn on the overhead light, and read everything that I have said about myself, borrowed from mouths of strangers. I've re-moulded their insults into body-hate and I'll sit with this version of myself for hours before I finally leave to find the makeup wipes.

AA Meetings

It felt like friendship, a lunchtime support group
in the outdated bathrooms at the back of the building.

We unleashed our frustrations one by one and watched
them bounce about the tiled walls, tumbling down the toilets –

becoming lodged in the sinks. We took it in turns to compare
our hunger pains and dizzy spells; using a rating system

of zero to ten, scoring our desire to be beautiful –
always an eleven – and pitched it against our desire to eat.

When we called our parents we each told the same lie:
"I'll have dinner at Ana's house tonight."

This is where it started.

Skipping meals

I draw a chalk hopscotch grid on the ground
and write 'lunch' in the first box,
'breakfast' and 'dinner' in the following squares.

I repeat this pattern five times and throw
five stones, one after the other.
I outline a five-column chart in my notebook:

Monday I will skip breakfast; Tuesday I will skip
lunch; Wednesday I will skip…
I keep writing until my weekly meals are planned.

Learning new words

Today at school they taught me another new word:
Heffer, shouted across a classroom;

like a game of shot put, the insult landed heavy
on the closed lid of my desk and I studied it.

The strong pose of the H and the squat stance
of each e; the hunchbacks of the fs and the r.

I saw myself spread across the two syllables;
collected the word from my desk top to stash it away

in the pocket of my jeans. I'll find it later,
and with a hand point chisel I'll draw the letters

onto the taught skin of over-sized upper thighs –
their insults rewritten as thinspiration.

Eating enough

I told a lot of lies about eating
at friends' houses,
having lunches at school,
being so stressed about exams
that I couldn't bring myself to snack.

When my mother hugged me too close
and rubbed her hands over
protruding shoulder-blades,
she'd always ask:
"Are you eating?"

"I'm eating enough,"
I always spoke back and she
always avoided responding.
"Enough is a relative term."
My future therapist will one day tell me.

Progress

Six months ago, I couldn't balance
a paracetamol capsule on my clavicle.

I don't know my waist to hip ratio,
but today I balanced an ibuprofen

in the dip between my shoulder and my neck –
and I held it there to the scales and back.

I try to balance two tablets and when I can't,
I write this down as my next milestone.

Your current balance is –

My friend suggests a cake or crumpet;
when I tell her that I can't afford either she offers to sub me.
I don't want to explain to her that she's using a different currency.

In my head I keep a running total:
-84 for breakfast
-20 for the five cereal bites that I will pass off as lunch
-76 for that ice-cream

I have to keep at least 500 for dinner or I will be accused of starving.
I decline the crumpet and ignore the lemon cake.
"I have a big dinner planned," I lie,
using reason number 17 for not eating.

From one extreme

In our house they're still called cheat days.
In reality they are we-promise-not-to-micro-manage-everything-we-eat days,
but the former is much catchier.

In the shower I plan breakfast,
over breakfast I plan lunch and afternoon snacks, and I'll ask:
"What takeaway does everyone fancy?" any time after noon.

When the weekend comes I'm incomplete
unless eating, grazing, binging on everything that I've wanted
all week but couldn't bring myself to purchase.

When I go the supermarket to buy chocolate,
crisps, pizza, ice-cream, bread, cheddar cheese spread
and crackers, I buy laxatives too.

Because in our house they're still called cheat days,
and every day is a micro-manage-everything-I-eat day –
the only difference is how many tablets I take before bed.

Diversion tactics

I dry my hair, dress myself, paint my nails –
start again. I strip my nails back to the base colour and re-paint them
a slightly different shade. I'm a better person when I'm busy.

I cure the nail varnish for eight minutes longer than necessary;
under the UV light I inspect the creases
of my knuckles for crumbs.

After this I will work for ten hours before I go home,
have a bath, read a book, go to bed, go to sleep,
on an empty stomach.

Denial

I don't take the doctor seriously when she says it.
On the sofa at home I tell my partner:
"Only skinny people have eating disorders."

"What about the people who are eating themselves to death?"

"They're different," I say, before explaining
again how eating disorders belong to the skinny,
not the formerly-fat or the trying-to-be-thin.

He asks me to eat something: a chocolate biscuit,
piece of fruit, slice of toast,
without adding the calories to my calculator.

We stay together on the sofa until my panic subsides.
I swear to call the number the doctor gave me,
and he promises he won't get the biscuits.

Mind over matter

She sits across the table from me and takes
my hand in hers before explaining:

"This is going to take willpower."
Still chewing garlic bread as she speaks.

She pries my jaw open and forces
the platitude in, before slamming my teeth together.

She mimes eating, bite by bite –
as though I need to be reminded of chewing.

I swallow down the urge to ask how much willpower
she thinks it takes to starve when you are hungry.

Aging the problem
Or: Eating my feelings

From my late-teens through to my early-twenties,
when feelings became too big for me
I would simply eat them.

I'd take huge bites of guilt and chew it together
with self-pity, and when their salt dried out
my insides I'd wash them down with chocolate milk.

Anger would be sandwiched inside a cheese-topped
roll and covered in mayonnaise –
because I didn't know how many calories were in mayonnaise.

Love came in the form of chocolate and cake,
and when I grew old enough
I discovered that chocolate was the food of loss too.

(In fact, chocolate is the food of most things.)

When I admit this to my therapist at the age of twenty-five,
I realise this problem that I don't think is a problem
is about ten years older than I didn't think it was.

Group therapy

"Doesn't it blow your mind?" she asks
the entire room, and gives us a minute
to process the information.

It does blow my mind,
but I can't openly agree with her
for fear of judgement, for fear

of encouraging bad thinking,
for fear that other people's minds
are intact and this realisation

is not actually as big as I think,
as she thinks, it is. But seconds pass,
and the "Yes" moves in a wave

around our safe circle. Even the leader –
our long-suffering deity – admits it blows
her mind too, that there are people out there

who can eat anything they want
without worrying about it.

Recovery position

Like physiotherapy, they give me exercises.
Stand in front of the mirror for a minute each morning
and find something to love –
write something positive on your body –
remind yourself that you're trying your best.

The muscles of my mouth ache from chanting
their affirmations, from chewing
over self-made compliments. But I still double
over, place my head between my knees
and tell myself that I am beautiful.

An apology to my body

I'm the one that has deprived food and water
because I'll be a pound lighter after the third pee of the morning.

I'm the one that takes more than the recommended dose
for another round of self-induced stomach flu.

I'm the one that wears Spanx under the size-ten-dress
to hide the outlines of my empty skin.

I'm the one that's spent years hating you,
even though you've never done anything but hold me.

Body, I'm sorry now and I hope it's not too late.

Number of days since –

A contagious anxiety preludes the announcement;
when I start to speak you look scared.

> "I haven't weighed myself so far this week."

You pause, check the calendar to see where we are;
to see why I think this is important.

> "I'm really proud of you,"

you say, when you mean to say you're relieved,
and I tell you that I'm proud too.

I hold in the part about how these three days have been
the longest ones so far this year.

Progress – Part two

Twelve months ago, I kept my stash of saved pills
in the dips between my shoulders and my neck.

Today, drying my hair in the mirror, I notice
I'm not thinner now but fuller. Clavicles can be seen

but they aren't piercing the surface and that's fine.
Dinner is in my belly and there's cake waiting for after,

and that's fine. I bullet-point all of the fine things.
When I see my therapist, I'll tell her these new truths.

Group therapy – Part two

"And I ate the whole thing," she says to the room
full of people who are sitting, mouths agape,
imagining the cake from her story.

She tells us that she hasn't even got to the best part
and we wipe away spittle, urge her to continue
so we can (ch)eat vicariously.

She licks her lips, exhales slowly and says:
"I didn't even feel guilty about it."
Her smile is sugar-white and sweet.

Our applause can be heard from two streets away.

If my body were a friend of mine

If you were a friend, and my behaviour
was that of your lover, I'd tell you to leave me.

Body, I can't count the ways in which I've wronged
you over the last nearly-three-decades.

If you were a friend, I'd be the friend you had to warn
other people about before introducing me.

Body, I'm sorry that on the days when people tore you
down I joined in instead of stopping them.

If you were a friend, I'd be the friend that made people ask
what it is you see in me; why you put up with my shit.

Body, I'll never know why you put up with my shit
but thank God that you have, that you do.

If you were a friend, I'd promise to change,
beg forgiveness, beg help, because changing isn't easy.

Body, thank you for holding out long enough
for change to still be an option.

1.6 million

We lie every day. Tell our friends that we're not
hungry, tell our partners, parents, lovers
that we're not hungry. Tell ourselves.

We're part of a growing statistic in a society
that harbours a need to be
more beautiful/more malnourished.

There are approximately 1.6 million people
in the UK living with a diagnosed,
or still-undiagnosed, eating disorder.

There are 1.6 million people in this country
who are starving themselves,
but it will take something more than food to fill us.

Epilogue

My belly is a swollen map of bad decisions
and dead-end relationships; a new road or river
stretched in every time I ate my feelings.

The skin around my stomach cost 120lbs; I use it
to store and carry shame, embarrassment,
and sometimes, even now, comfort food.

My favourite part of not being "fat" anymore is rejecting
the men who couldn't love me when I was;
my least favourite part of not being fat is looking
in the mirror and seeing fat where there is none;
seeing a body that takes up too much space in a world
that has conditioned me to be as small, as insignificant,
as palatable as possible to a patriarchy that teaches
fat and pretty as mutually exclusive.

If I could, I would use these loose-skinned arms,
launch myself from the top of those gloriously golden
(McDonald's) double arches and fly away from the stigma
that tells me anything that isn't green must taste
like guilt with a low-fat dressing.

...because when someone sits down to write your eulogy,
they will not care how much butter you did
or did not put on your crumpets.

Acknowledgements

A special thanks to the journals, and their editors, who featured some of these poems prior to publication. Thank you to: *Atrium* for publishing 'Diversion Tactics'; *Ink Sweat and Tears* for publishing 'Denial'; *Riggwelter Press* for publishing 'AA Meetings'; and *Picaroon Poetry*, who gave them all a forever home (and published one or two along the way).

A quiet thank you to anyone who has ever talked to me about food, their bodies, and their battles with both. You're beautiful. Please apply these poems as needed.

About the Author

Charley Barnes is the current Worcestershire Poet Laureate (2019-2020). She has written poems from a young age but – as her mum can verify – it's certainly a skill that has been honed over the years, rather than something that came naturally. Charley's work has since been featured in several poetry journals, including: *Riggwelter Press, Atrium,* and *Wordgathering.* Her debut pamphlet, *A Z-hearted Guide to Heartache,* was published by V. Press in 2018, and Charley used this to explore the themes of mental health, disability, and romantic relationships.

Body Talk is Charley's second pamphlet, that sees her discuss relationships with food and the body, culminating in an open discussion around eating disorders – including some of the harsh realities of suffering from one. While these poems may be hard to swallow, they will be – Charley hopes – a necessary pill.

In 2018, Charley graduated with her Doctorate degree in Creative Writing and since then she has been lecturing at various academic institutions around the West Midlands, most recently the University of Worcester and Newman University.

Charley publishes crime fiction under the moniker of C. S. Barnes; she manages Sabotage Reviews and, subsequently, co-ordinates the acclaimed Saboteur Awards; and she occasionally sits down for tea and cake with some of her favourite humans (Charley plans to do more of this in the future).

Wherever you are along the journey, Charley hopes that these poems will be a gentle hug/a low-lit lamp/a nudge of encouragement/whatever you need.

L - #0226 - 300919 - C0 - 210/148/2 - PB - DID2633647